Serenity

Poetry by R. e. Taylor

Published by Shadowlight Publishing
11 Angelina Street, Macgregor, Queensland,
Australia 4109

All pictures from www.shutterstock.com

© 2013 R. e. Taylor

Dedication

Thank you L.W. for forcing me to leave the dark side and explore the world of the light and to all of my friends on Facebook who have done nothing but encouraged me from the beginning!

R. e.

If She Only Knew

Why can't I tell her?
I dream about her every second I sleep
My thoughts wrap around her in the days light
But she doesn't know
I could never tell her how I feel
She would not, could not understand
I watch her as she dances through life
Smiling and seeing only good
She is one of a kind
Truly an angel to be worshipped
She hides her wings to be among people
I know that she must have an idea
But I am not of her class
I am old, with the wrinkles of life
Too many beers in my youth
And eyes that don't see as well as they used to
However, my heart works
It aches when I think that she could be mine
Fighting the mind that knows better
So, I dream and I watch without speaking a word
Living with the hope that she could be mine
Living with the knowledge that she could never be.

That Beautiful Pain

That beautiful pain
The one that lives in my heart
Born the minute you leave
It takes away my sleep
Ripping my dreams apart
That beautiful pain
The one that only I know
I can never share it
Not that I would if I could
No one would ever understand
They do not see you as I do
That beautiful pain
The one that only fades when you return
Would I live without it?
Could I live without it?
Not if it meant that I would never had met you
That beautiful pain
I would rather suffer
Dealing with the hurt
Rather than lose you
And give the pain to another.

A Single Tear

Trying to hold it back
It is too hard especially with a broken heart
A single tear flows down my cheek
Telling the world of my sadness
What mistakes I made
Ones that I cannot change
Words I said
Others I should have said
Yet others I could have said but didn't
Raging in my memory
They tear at my soul
Trying to escape to release the pain
Years, decades they try while they rip me apart
Finally every words is released
Not in a flood
Not in a torrent
But in a single tear flowing down my cheek.

The Frozen Pathway to Your Heart

I never could find the way
It is a path few have traveled
If you ever allowed anyone
The path is treacherous
Full of pitfalls and deep valleys
I don't think anyone made it all the way
You'd ever leave an opening
Not even the slightest crack
Cold winds blow out from the valley
Covering the path with ice and frost
Hiding the footprints
Covering the bodies of those who came before
The few who made it this far
Not knowing the right words
The right actions
They gave up hope
Not knowing that over the next hill
Just beyond the clouds
Lies a door with a golden lock
Waiting for a young knight
To have the right words
Only then the paths will thaw
The winds will warm
The walls will crack
The lock to you heart will open
And maybe once again
You'll let someone love you
And maybe once again
You will be able to love again.

Jackie

Doing 85 in a 35
Driving my daddy's El Camino
The engine roars like a hungry lion
A creature that would never be tamed
The wheels throw dust behind me
There is a brunette on the seat beside me
Daisy dukes and a halter top
Aphrodite has come to life
Her legs wrap around my stick shift
She takes it from first to fifth
Ever gaining speed on this country back road
Fence posts rush by in a blur
I can hear no sounds except the wheels
Tearing up the road as we fly over it
So many accidents on this road
So many people killed on "Dead Man's Curve"
What makes me think I can make it?
Is the chance worth the love of a girl?
Would I ever get a night with her
Or even a kiss?
The speedometer hits 110
The stars are no longer points of light in a distance sky
They begin whirling they are so beautiful
She moves closer to me
Her skin glistens in the light from the dashboard
Beads of moisture looks like a million diamonds
The song on the radio is pounding into my body
Building ecstasy far beyond what any boy should feel
Stopping can cause the feelings to wither and die
The faster we go the more erotic she feels
Her every nerve controls her passion

Burning deep within her ivory skin
Bringing her to the edge of orgasm
The brakes lock
The tires squeal as she screams in passion
The motor dies with a bang
The wheels stop in total quiet
Then there is just silence
The silence was broken by her voice
She told me her name was Jackie
Then the door opened as she disappeared
Was she just in my mind?
An image conjured from my loneliness?
The motor died next to a tree
A white cross stood before me
Surrounded by dying flowers.

30 Years Gone

Such a long time to be apart
No contact, but you are still in my heart
Memories of the years we spent together
The smiles, the laughs
The times we made love under a warm summer sun
It was paradise
The best times of my life
One misunderstanding between us
No one at fault ended us
Destroyed paradise
The smiles and laughs died in a single day
And the summer love making
Faded into a distant memory
I still look at your picture in an old yearbook
Torn and tattered age is trying to take that from me too
But you will always be in my thoughts
You will always be in my heart
I will always love you
I just wish I could tell you one time.

Glass Heart

Such a fragile organ
A heart made of glass
Born pure and flawless
Filled with undying love
It ages with cracks and flaws
Some visible to the naked eye
Some so small they cannot be seen
Every heart of glass breaks
Shatters deep within the soul
Shards can never be replaced
The broken heart can never be fixed
it simply dies a painful death
At least it can feel no pain.

If Only

Time passes so fast
It leads us to an unknown future
While the past is lost in a flash
There is no chance to fix mistakes
Say the words that should have been said
Retrieve a love that was lost
Memories fade to dust
New ones take their place
Why can't we go back even for an hour?
Why can't we know then what we know now?
We suffer with choices that shouldn't have been made
Just one moment could change your life
One word said in the spur of the moment
One kiss that should have been shared
One love that would have lasted forever
If you could go back would you make the changes
Would you let the past stay the same?
If only time was like crossing the street
What a difference a second could be
If only...

Lost Dreams

A thousand days and a thousand nights
I have dreamt of you.
Your smile, your scent, your voice floods my senses
As do the wind the rain and the warmth of the sun.
It is not my way to say what my heart has screamed
every time we speak.
It is not my way to tell you that the touch of your hand
Your soft gentle kiss goodbye fills my soul with light
My heart fills with joy and love
Only to lose it once again, into the past when your door
closes behind you.
My life falls back into a bottomless pit
Where I eternally dwell and dream for that one moment
That one second, the forever when my hand brushes yours
Our lips touch ever so slightly
And I will finally be able to say what is in my heart.

If She Remembers Me

I sit on a cold park bench
The sun is shining
The air is warm
My loneliness chills me to the bone
Thoughts wandering
Wondering what my life is for
I thought I knew
The one day I met her I was sure
It was meant for a brown-haired angel
The one to whom I offered my heart
Who sent it back without a thought
She doesn't know what she has done
How far into the darkness she has driven me
Maybe she will learn from my words
And when I am gone
She will shed but a single tear
If she even remembers me.

Hidden By A Blue Sky

Sky
Light blue
Eternal
Mixing colors
A prism united
Hiding endless darkness
Worlds orbiting distant stars
Innumerable living planets
Will they be intelligent like us?
Does their blue sky allow them to know us?

Fractals

Colors, strands and beams
Arranged into a rainbow
Twisted around each other
They form a warped vision
Every piece large
Every piece small
Connected in an infinite web
Confusion and clarity
Chaos and order
All in one place
Spread across the Universe
Conjured up in nightmares
Just a series of mathematical equations
Numbers in the right place at the right time
Creating such beauty.

Ripples In A Pond

A small stone
Tossed by a child into a still pond
The water splashes
Ripples move outward touching the shore
The rock falls to the bottom
It joins a million others just like it
The water smoothes to what it was
Did the child change the pond?
Did the stone make any difference?
Is everything just as it was before?
Even the smallest thing can make a change
That pond will never be exactly the same
Even if they cannot be seen there are changes
The water is a little bit deeper
There is a new piece of stone to join the others
Even the fish have less area to swim
Absolutely nothing is the same
If a single stone can change an entire ecosystem
What do you think a single idea could do
Once it makes its own ripples.

The Ballerina

Watching her dancing
It is hard to believe that she was that little girl
Barely able to stand on her toes
She struggled to keep time with the music
Her pink tutu swirling around
Twisting around her legs
She looked like a ballerina
But she danced like a crash test dummy
Years past as she grew
Matured into a young woman of ten
She took the stage at her seventh recital
Leaping and dancing across the stage
It was hard to imagine that she was the same girl
That clumsy little girl
The daughter who made me laugh when she danced
She was a practiced artist
Graceful and poised
She was not my little Elizabeth
She was a ballerina and she was happy

Please Take Me Back

Will someone take me back to the river
I lived and loved on her shores
Her sand, her rocks were my friends
Her trees and the wind rustling through the leaves
were my music.
I saw thousands of words in her flowers
A thousand dreams and wishes came from her rocks
Many days I dozed in the mists of her waterfall
I swam in her currents, each of which she gave to relax me
Many had known her before me, I know that
Her caves and rocks held the lives of people long gone
They too must have dreamed with her
They must have seen the same things I see
They too found hope in her waves
The melody of her water must have charmed them
Her life, the one she gladly shared with them, brought
them through their hard times
She always helped me through my hunger
My pain and loneliness
Now I am an old man with an old man's dreams
Before I die and I am forgotten
I will ask only one thing of those who love me.
Please...take me back to the river.

Birdsong

Skies of the brightest blue
Uncluttered by pollutions
Birds circle overhead
Looking for a place to roost
Males with their bright colors
Looking for a mate for the spring
Chirping into the cool valley air
Songs of greetings and invitations
They echo off the trees and mountains
Combining into a symphony
Males and females meet
They sing and dance into the early evening
Joining together in an ancient ritual
And life begins again.

Mother Nature's Canvas

Mother Nature's canvas
Endless blue sky
Unchanging
She waves her brush
Such beautiful strokes
Moved by her breathe
They drift across her canvas
Lit by the sun
They become a masterpiece
Even though they may try
No artist could ever paint such beauty
No picture could ever match her work
Mother Nature should be proud
The world below looks up in awe
She has created such perfection
Using just a brush and her breath
That is a miracle to be admired.

The Magic Of The Veiled Valley

I look into the valley
A shroud of mist hides its beauty
Pale and gray it hangs below me
The sun has yet to reach down from its heights
There is the smell of a million flowers
Floating on cool breezes
Cooled by a shallow blue/green pond
Rising from the distant floor
The sounds of chirping birds
Chicks crying for food from their mothers
Hawks scream while they look for food
Flying high above the valley's sides
They echo from stony walls covered with vines
The only sounds on a tranquil spring day
The mist breaks for just second
Leaving a trail of swirls and eddies
As a spotted fawn runs across the dewy grass
The sun rises dissolving the morning's veil
The animals hide
The birds nest to raise their young
The beauty of the valley is still there
But the magic that was hidden by the fog
The illusion of that peaceful world
The melodic song of the valley's life
Burns away in the sun's bright glare
Maybe tomorrow morning before the sun rises
I will again stand on this rocky outcropping
I will see the veiled world
And the magic will be there again.

Treasure Of The Sands

It is truly amazing
Seashells washed upon the shore
It is hard to believe that it started as something's home
I wonder what happened to the animal that created it
Such beautiful colors and patterns
Rainbows of color painted into a small space
Did they know that they were creating beauty?
Did they know that women would kill to wear their shells?
Such beauty from creatures
That live on the bottom of the sea
Neptune was gracious enough to share his treasure
Treasure anyone can find Found
on the gentle sands Shining in
the warm midday sun It is truly
amazing.

Beauty Of The Solar Winds

Solar winds
Dangerous and deadly
Launched by a living yellow star
Invisible they wrap around distant planets
Radiating the atmosphere
Producing rainbows of vibrant colors
Such beauty held at bay by a thick atmosphere
The beings of the planets look to their heavens
In wonder and amazement they stare
Praising their god for such a sight
They do not know how close they are
How close their extinction is to happening
They do not think of that
They do not think of their own mortality
They do not thank their gods
They do not thank them for a chance that occurred billions of years ago
The Fates gave their world the right composition
The right make up of gases and rocks
The solar winds pass them by
And all they have is a beautiful sky
To look at on a clear night
To fall in love under
To sleep under in a restful sleep
All they know is that their gods gave them nocturnal beauty
And that is all they need to know
All they want to know
They just see the beauty.

That Old Willow Tree

A place of solitude
Down by the swamp
A willow tree grows among the weeds
Branches reach to the sky
Fronds hang down reaching for the earth below
Birds live and sing in her branches
Shade loving plants grow at her feet
It is so pleasant on a hot August afternoon
The perfect place to just sit and think
Maybe paint a beautiful landscape
Or even an inspired poem
Such a place exists only for the artist
There aren't many in our hectic world
They have been paved over
Polluted so that the beauty is long gone
Or just lost to everlasting progress
If you find a place like that old willow tree
Love it and go there for moments of solitude
Think about what nature has given you for that day
Because tomorrow it may be gone
And you may sit at the foot of a parking meter
But it will never be the same.

God Isn't My Landlord

I am so tired
I tried to sleep
I truly did but it evaded me
There is snoring in the other room
How I long to be sharing that bed
Waiting for a dream to start
Instead I sit here at my computer
The TV is the only on the house still awake
An old-time gospel preacher is on asking for money
What does he need money for?
Doesn't God provide for him?
Or won't God give him credit to live on
Maybe God is his landlord and he is behind on his rent
What am I thinking?
God couldn't be a landlord
Where would the rent checks be delivered?
Maybe after I write one more chapter
Or maybe just another sentence
Perhaps just one more word
Any word
Then I might be able to sleep
And in my dreams
I won't care the God owns that preacher's house
Not that it matters anyway
He isn't my landlord
I know where to send my rent checks.

The Poet

We have been around for thousands of years
Reading our words for kings and queens
and a few people who gathered just to hear us talk.
We lived on the copper coins they could afford
Traveled through the lands
Writing what we saw, dreams and thoughts.
Our words were put to music and made immortal
Others were acted on the stage
Making people laugh and cry.
Some words changed the way people thought
Ended hatred between people
People who should not feel hate.
People died because they did not realize what
our words could do
Many times a love bogged in fear was loosed
This because of a few words we wrote.
God only knows how many children our words
have brought smiles to and how many starting
thinking because of what we wrote.
Why do we do it?
Not to end wars or hatred
Not for the lovers who found each other because of us
Not even for the copper coins people throw
We do it because we love words
We do it to share our feelings
We do it so that someday maybe someone
Will read our thoughts, dreams and words
And they will be remembered long after we are gone.

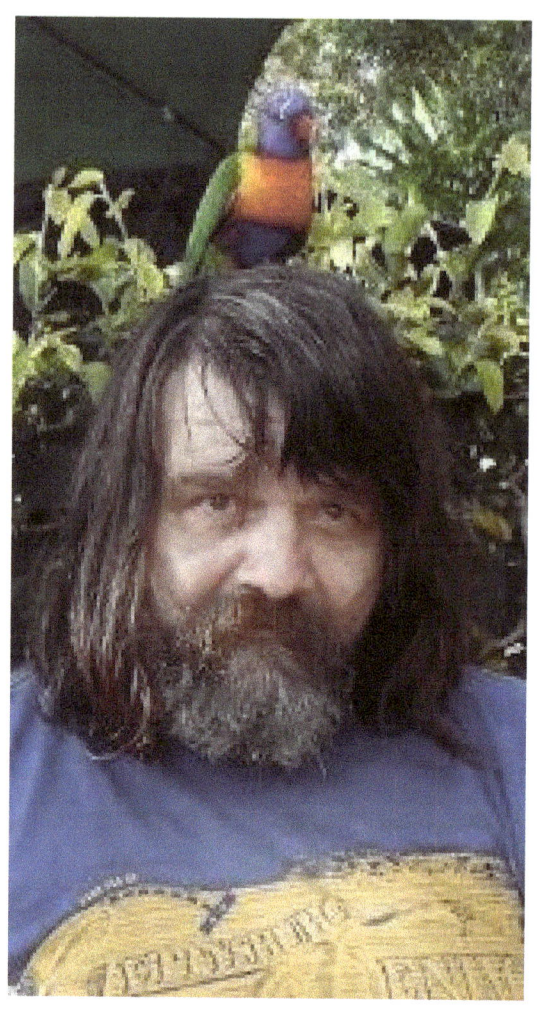

I Am Trebor

Who am I?
My name is Robert
It was given to me
I didn't choose it
It is a common name
Too common
No true identity of its own
There are a thousand who share it with me
If my name were different
Not as common
Would I be different?
Could another name make me smarter
More creative?
Or better looking?
I never had the chance to find out
I was named after another
He named me after him
Hoping that maybe I would be like him
I was not like him
I could not be like him
It was always as if I saw things differently
My world was not his black and white
I observed
I questioned
I saw colors, words and rhythm in everything
I was the opposite of him
Maybe he should have named me Trebor?
Then my life, my vision, my name
Would never be shared with anyone.

The Purple Flaming Banana

Reading a new poem
Written late night
While fighting to sleep
Trying to stay awake
Finished as the sun rises above a distant mountain
Purple Flaming Banana
I look around and see people
Their eyes glazed over in confusion
What is the poem about?
Does it have a deep, hidden meaning?
Is the purple flaming banana love?
Does it mean anger, hatred or a twisted mind?
Was I on drugs?
Did I have way too much to drink?
What is the meaning of the purple flaming banana?
It was not love
It was not hate or anger
What was the meaning of a purple flaming banana?
It was just that
Nothing special
Nothing unique
Just a purple flaming banana
Nothing more.

One Great Poem

One poem
Just the right words
The right sounds
Combined in the right fashion
To share an idea
A dream I have deep in my soul
I have written many poems
I have used many words where the sounds were right
They were not perfect
They were not great
Before I die I want to write that one poem that will be remembered
In my fifty years I have heard a million words
I have seen thousands of beautiful things
My eyes have wept
My thoughts have traveled through a world unknown
I have loved only once but my heart has died a hundred times
My name will be forgotten
My dreams will never be shared
Time grows short
My mind falters as the light in my eyes fade
The last thought I have as my soul leaves my body
I never found the right words
I never found the right sounds
I never wrote that one great poem
A virus took it all away from me
Took me away
I will never be remembered.

Write Things Down

What am I going to write?
Is has been hours without an idea
The sun cast the last of its light hours ago
There is no moon to shine in the cold night
The stars are blocked by late summer clouds
Music is missing from the radio
Some politician is droning on trying to save his job
I had so many thoughts earlier in the day
Why didn't I write them down?
My mind is blank as the clock strikes four
My eyes strain and my head aches in the dim light
Ideas are just avoiding my efforts to find them
Why didn't I write things down like I should?
My eyes close and I drift off to sleep
Tomorrow is another day
I know I will have ideas about what to write
I will remember to write them down
Tomorrow night I will be able to write
If I just remember to write things down.

Those Three Words

I was walking down the street
It was a sunny day until clouds came
And it started to rain, not a gentle rain
The drops felt like clubs as they beat against me
Outside the school I found a notebook
Just a group of paper tied together by a steel spring
There was nothing special about it
I had seen thousands of them before
However this one drew my attention
For a moment it was all I could think about.
Would they need it today
Or was it the one they doodled in
When the class was dull
The cover had writing on it
The letters covered the black cardboard
I needed to know
Was it their wisdom, their dreams
Or some mathematical equation
I would simply not understand.
I picked it up.
It was nearly soaked but it stood strong
Protecting whatever was inside.
I opened it expecting something, but I was afraid
For fear that I may be disappointed
The pages were blank except for the first one
It had just three words "What is it?"
I put the notebook back.
Those three words, those three simple words haunted
me the rest of the day
I never found out what it was
But after that day I never stopped asking.

My Pledge

I pledge my life to what is sacred
Not one deity or Supreme Being
Not to an idea that I am told I should follow
Not to the words of an ordained minister
Not to thoughts printed in a leather bound book
Not to commandments carved in ancient stones
I pledge my life to what is sacred
To the spirits that exist in everything the universe has to offer
To the beauty of a blue sky with flowing clouds
To the first breath of a new born child
To the opening flower after a long cold winter
To the timeless Earth on which we stand
I pledge my life to what is sacred
To every rock plant and animal of the woods
To the wind as it blows down a sloping valley
To the lifeless moon that lights the night
To the sun that lights the day
To what brings peace into my life
I pledge my life to what is sacred
I pledge myself to life..

Where Does Time Go?

Where does the time go?
December becomes June
Spring and winter become one
Seasons of snow merge with times of rain
Night comes before the day
Plants are born, die and are re-born
Without the chance to bloom or go to seed
Mountains worn down by tidal streams
Become gravel at the feet of new peaks
Born from pressures unseen, unknown
Time twists and warps around reality
Changing what is seen and what is known
Time…once a constant
Flowing in eddies and currents
Down steep peaks lined with sharp edges
It flows while we watch and ask
Where does time go?

Deciding

I think too much Wondering
what I can do What I could
have done better What I
shouldn't have done
Possibilities run though my mind
Making the pulse beat in my head
It is so hard
So many different realities
So many different ending for each beginning
Why didn't I think when it was happening?
Maybe things moved to fast
Maybe I knew somehow that I would never decide
Turn right and buy a pizza
Turn left and meet the girl I was fated to marry
Go straight and get hit by that blue Cadillac
What should I have done?
Maybe I should just give up and live
Let the fates decide for me
That way I don't have to decide and I can live
Yes, I can live without deciding how my life will go
It will be my decision that I won't decide
I'll decide just to live.

Downtown

Dirt, cobblestone, brick and asphalt
Trodden on by horses, kids and others
Driven over by buggy, streetcar and automobile
Past shops, restaurants and theaters
It was the center of a town
A place where life took place
Couples who had their first dates
A child who sees their first movie
People who worked the shops
They were all part of the memories
They made the history that we remember
Now, the shops are gone
The restaurants have become rundown or closed
Converted into ghetto bars with all of the crime
The theaters died when the multiplex was born
Sixteen screens each without a personality
The beautiful architecture of the past has been replaced
Carved marble changed into sheets of sterile glass
It disappeared as the world progressed
At least the Downtown of the past still lives
The couples, the child and the people remember
And as long as they do...there will always be a
Downtown.

An Offline Hello

Whatever happened to hello?
Meeting and shaking hands
That moment of sharing yourself
That was a big part of life
There were no strangers
Just friends you haven't met
Conversation used as an ice breaker
Learning more about the person as you spoke
That was an eternity ago
Before the invent of smart phones
Constant contact with the internet
Naked pictures , and Facebook pages
Embarrassing videos from when you were a teen
Slander and gossip posted in a moment of anger
A million pages of someone with the same name
Not all of it true
But it must be since it is on the web
One time let's go back to the old days
Meet face to face not screen to screen
Forget that you have the ability to text
Sit down and just talk
Get to know each other
Take time to learn their history and mysteries
For once don't look them up on-line
The real person is so much better
They just want a simple hello.

We Are Just Human

So many words to describe a person
White, black, brown, yellow and red
African American, Caucasian, Latino, Asian, Arab
Blonde, brunette, redhead
So many words
Many words are said with hatred and ignorance
Created by men with small minds
They are meant only to embarrass and hurt
Passed down through the generations
They are still used by those who do not understand
Those who fear our differences
However, even with all our differences
There is only one word which truly fits
It fits our different nationalities
The differences in the pigments in our skin
Despite everything we are all humans
No more, no less
Just humans.

Through The Eyes Of A Child

Eyes of the deepest brown
They look at a world in a fresh way
Seeing snow and rainbows for the first time
She smiles in wonder at everything
Everything age has tarnished
She is so innocent and pure Full
of love and beauty Everything we
forgot as we grew
Should we take the time to look back?
Look at snow as nature's magic
Should we say ah when we see a rainbow
We could watch in amazement at a cloud
Imagining a bunny floating across the sky
Maybe we should look through her eyes
See what she sees
If only we could see it as a child does
Then the world would be a beautiful place.

Alone On The Stage

She stands on the stage alone
A single light bulb shines on her face
Lined and wrinkled by years of smiles and tears
It shows a life full of emotions
She's cried
She's laughed
She has been royalty
She has been a pauper
She's even died a time or two
Once or twice she felt love in lines written by others
Millions of words
Thousands of people feeling what she felt
Theaters sold out
Now she stands on the stage
Looking at empty seats
She is a nobody
Her name is no longer known
She is alone on the stage
Looking into the empty room
Through empty eyes
Thinking about her now empty life
She lives off her memories
Memories of what was
Memories of what could have been
For the first time she cries
and there is no one to see it.

Don't Forget To Dance

Dancing to a 4/4 beat
The rhythm takes over our souls
There are no enemies
Just friends sharing the moment
The music affects everyone
Regardless of sex. color or creed
Everyone is having fun
It doesn't matter what the song is
Listen to the music
Feel the rhythm rush through your body
Don't take the time to hate
Take the time to listen, dance and enjoy
Live your life to the rhythms you hear
The days will be brighter
The nights will be more exciting
Just live the beat
and don't forget to dance.

Rainbows

So many colors follow a rain
Beautiful shades of all colors
Children know of rainbows
Their eyes reflect their wonder
They know it is the home of fairies
Pots of gold left by their owners
So many things of a child's dream
Innocently they watch the skies
They beg their mommies and daddies
Asking to climb over that last hill
To take them to the end of the rainbow
It is a place of miracles
A place of imagination adults don't understand
Children have been watching rainbows forever
God made them for children to feel hope
To know that He loves them
To know that a scary storm has ended
Adults should look at rainbows with a child's eyes
Just accept its beauty
Realize that it is the homes of fairies
Take time to look for that pot of gold
Look through their eyes and see what children see
It is no longer a simple rainbow
It is a place of miracles
It is a place where you can find your imagination
It is happiness.

Fairy

The tiniest of creatures
Born of dreams
They life in fantasies
Born with lacy wings
As sheer as a spring breeze
They make no sound
The creatures die as we grow
Logic takes over for fantasy
Fairies no longer have a place
Our lives have changed
Remember for one brief moment
Think back to when you were a child Look at
that flower growing in your yard Look
carefully through the eyes of innocence A
fairy will be there laughing and dancing
Leaping between the petals
All you have to do is shed reality
And see another world A
world that you forgot All
you have to do is look.

The White Pumpkin

A farmer tends his field
Vines grow and wrap around each other
Giant white flowers bloom in the heat of summer
Butterflies and bees dance from flower to flower
Spreading the pollen from male to female
Inseminating to create the next generation
Weeks later the children arrive
They laugh and giggle
As they run among the orange pumpkins
Each one takes their favorite home for carving or pie
One pumpkin is small, oddly shaped with a white skin
It sits alone by the wooden fence as the rest are taken
The day before Halloween one child comes for a visit
Out of the dozens of pumpkins still waiting
The child chose the small white one
His parents point out all the beauty around him
The child doesn't change his mind or his heart
He spoke of the one he wanted
"This one is like me," he said
As he lifted it into his wheelchair
That was all that had to be said
The white pumpkin was loved by a little boy
A boy who knew what it was like to be different
He knew what it was like to be loved
And now, so did that small, oddly shaped pumpkin
with a white skin.

Daddy's Little Girl

I was there when your eyes first saw the world
You were Daddy's little girl
You grew, changed
When you fell from your tricycle
A small scrape
I kissed your tears away
You told me that you met a boy
Sitting behind you in first grade
He pulled your ponytail
He teased you
Told the other boys stories about you
Then finally he kissed you
He stayed with you
When you were in trouble
When you had that bad year when you were 17
Even when you hated him
Telling him you never wanted to see him again
He stayed
He told you how much he loved you
Now I look at you
Daddy's little girl
All grown and lovely
I see your tears though your thin white veil
They are not mine to kiss away
He is here for you
He will be the one to take your pain away
And he will kiss away your tears
From this day forward.

Shampoo And Beer

It has been so many years
You left without a word
I cried, I begged but you didn't care
Many nights I reached for you
You weren't there
I sit alone in a darkened room
The windows closed
A soft amber light glows in the corner
But it doesn't cast shadows
The scent of shampoo and beer fills my senses
I remember your hair
The memory burnt in my mind decades ago
Brown and long It
was your scent
Shampoo and beer
It makes me think
Makes me remember
Our fist kiss
The summers in the sun
The times we made love
The leaves below us
The stars above
Our talks about having children
Our lives together
How can the thought of you bring those memories back?
You left so long ago
All I have left are my dreams
And the scent that I know
The scent that I love
Shampoo and beer.

Waiting For the Phone to Ring

Waiting by the phone
Hoping it will ring
Maybe she will call
It has been way too long
We spoke every day
Tying up the phones for hours
We would never run out of things to say
Nonsensical mutterings
Romantic words shared in poetic verse
The phone sits in total silence
A deafening silence
Way too loud to be ignored
Waiting is the hardest part
Not knowing what is going on the other end
I miss hearing her voice as she sings her words
If only the phone would ring I could be happy
Maybe, just maybe I should marry her?
Could she have broken up with me?
I just don't (do not) know because that damn phone won't ring
I will wait and wait for as long as it takes
But before I do that
Before I suffer the pain of staring at the phone
I had better check to see
I need to know what is happening
I need to move that switch and turn the ringer on
Then I will sit, I will wait until the phone rings.

The Light Of Diana

The darkness of the midnight sky
A blessing of the gracious gods of Olympus
The most holy Diana travels across the sky in a glittering chariot
The waning crescent moon a slight sliver of Diana's shield, shows her protecting bow
Keeping the innocent safe
For the moment when Venus can bless their being
She keeps safe the hearts of women who do not wish to be loved
Her light keeps the spirited god Cupid at bay until the desire for love proves itself
As she travels, lovers look up making wishes to her and they see her being
She leaves sparking jewels in her wake
For those whose wishes are to be granted
Red and blue and white they twinkle in the blackness of nothingness
However, I, a mere mortal am the most grateful to the night's dim light
It is by Diana's light that I look at your flawless beauty
Watch you as you sleep with dreams that make you smile as no person can
She is the one who keeps your tears away while allowing mine to flow
When Diana travels far beyond the distant horizon and Apollo rises in the east
For a pair of fortnights I shall fade back into the world where you and I would never meet
I will fade back and wait until
Diana once again shows her light.

Until I can again see your beauty in her silvery light
I shall feel a love which cannot be returned
Such is the blessing and the curse of Diana and her magical light

Two Warrior Hearts

Two warrior hearts
Beating separately
The sound is deafening
Telling all other hearts to stay away
They have been alone for so long
Fighting different battles
Under a dark moon they meet
The stars fade away as they get closer
Their beating is the same
Sounding as if they are just one heart
One heart wounds the other
The other hearts wounds the first
Cutting a vein in each other's hands
The weaker heart beats even stronger
That night they shared the sting of blood
Such passion erupts without a word
The two hearts become one
They are united for all time
They are not married
They are bound by blood
A stronger bond cannot be found
A Klingon love is eternal
As it should be when two warrior heart meet.

As I Lie Beside You...

As I lie beside you
I look at you sleeping
The twinkling of candle's golden light
The sound of the clock down the hall
Chimes in another hour
A melodic tone in an otherwise silent night
Your smile shows that you are in another world
What are you dreaming?
Maybe I don't want to know
Maybe it is a memory we already shared
It may be a dream of something yet to come
I know that what ever it is
It makes you happy
Should I give you a kiss?
Awake you just to tell you of my love
No, I shall not bring you back to this world
Relive that one memory that makes you smile
Hope for the dream yet to come
I shall let you sleep
When the candle has long since died
The sun has risen and shines into your eyes
Only then will I tell you of my love
And maybe, you will tell me of your dream.

The Thin Violet Thread

A thin violet thread
Barely noticeable
Light reflects off the shiny edges
Flashing tiny stars into the air
Winding its way from the dresser
Hard to see
Yet easy to notice
It tickles your feet as you walk
A breeze blows by
Lifting it from the floor
Swirling it around
It dances and twists at your feet
The lightness The
softness Caresses
you skin
Twisting around your toes
You smile
Then you think
The thread started somewhere
Looking, following, seeking
Your baby
Playing
Unwinding, thread by thread
You watch
Tears start to form
As your best shirt fades into a memory
And the baby looks at you and smiles
Suddenly that shirt doesn't matter
And once again that thread swirls,
dances and tickles
And you laugh.

A Bluish Violet Flower

A bluish violet flower watches from the shore of an ancient riverbed
A river born of fire when the Earth was new
Sulfuric air, ground ripped apart from Earth's upheaval
Chemicals mixed with lightening to create life
Single celled animals and ancient reptiles
And a single plant on the burnt earth
A single plant with a single bluish violet flower
It lived its life with cooling water
A million flowers bloomed every spring
Fish and turtles swam in its currents
Children played on its shore
Laughing and jumping into the refreshing waters
The waters caressed the bluish violet flower
Giving it life saving moisture
Still the bluish violet flower watched the fish, the turtles and the children
The river long ago died
The riverbed that held life, is still now
Rocks of sandstone create a natural blanket
The only fish are fossils of life millions of years old
That bluish violet flower
The one whose life began when time was young
The one who watched when life began and thrived in a lonely riverbed
It remembers the fish, the turtles, the children and the flowers
That bluish violet flower still watches
It watches the stillness and the silence
And all alone it mourns

Darling Alexis

Born in the dead of winter you warmed our hearts
Eyes filled with innocence you looked on your new world
We waited for you to come
We had hopes for you but you filled our wildest dreams
You were born helpless and small
But even then you had power over those who met you
You owned the world the minute you were born
As you own our every heartbeat
Alexis you will grow and be a beautiful woman
Your life will be full of dreams and hopes of your own
You will set the destiny you choose
Yet, you will be a woman with a heart full of love
Until then we will love you and protect you
Teach you how to be the person you should be
Even after all those years we will remember when you were born
That cold winter day when you came into our lives
The day you were born you changed us all and gave us hope
We learned what true love is just from seeing your eyes and your smile
Alexis thank you for being part of our lives.

You Own Me

You own my eyes
No matter where I look I see you
You own my thoughts
I cannot get you out of my head
You own my dreams
I see you in my arms as I drift off to sleep
You own my tongue
Words of my love for you flow forth whenever I speak
You own my heart
Every beat it beats is only for you
You own my breath
You take it away from me every time I think of you
You own my hopes
All of my wishes and hopes would be nothing without you
You own me and you don't even know it.

The Secret Of The Moon

The Moon sets in the west
Sinking below a distant horizon
Does she see the Moon rising in the East
Could there be a second in time
A second where we both look upon the same Moon
So far away her eyes look at the lonely sphere
Does she know the tears I shed looking at it
Dreaming that she is looking into her eyes
I may never know
The Moon is a silent mistress
Keeping her secrets from mortal man
Even the one of a woman's love
Yet, every night I will watch her float across the sky
I will dream that she is doing the same
While thinking of me, my heart and my love
That is the only wish I make under the light of the Moon
Maybe someday it will come true and she will see my love
The Moon with a secret that she may wish to share
And all will be made good under the gray light
And she will smile at the Moon and thank her.

Aged Beauty

Such aged beauty
Young so many years ago
Beauty that is only given by the gods
Time has taken its toll
Still your soul is that of a child
The love in your heart is that of a child
Pure and unlimited
That is all hidden
Makeup and hair dye hide the real woman
The one deep inside
The one with a warm loving heart
I have seen the real woman
Despite the ravages of age
The deep wrinkles on her face
The dark circles under her eyes
She is truly beautiful

www.ingramcontent.com/pod-product-compliance
Ingram Content Group UK Ltd.
Pitfield, Milton Keynes, MK11 3LW, UK
UKHW022122230426
12048UKWH00011BA/662